RETIREMENT ISN'T BORING

WHEN YOU LIVE IN AN ACTIVE ADULT COMMUNITY

Irene A. Hammond
with Leanne B. Martin

ISBN: 978-1-4834-7088-7 (sc)
ISBN: 978-1-4834-7087-0 (e)

Library of Congress Control Number: 2017909059

Lulu Publishing Services rev. date: 06/09/2017

"This is a great resource for this niche market supporting a partnership between the 55+ consumer and the real estate community"

Judy Lowe, Commissioner of
Arizona Department of Real Estate

"We went thru this book and took notes! Irene covers things we hadn't considered. Thank you for your insight".

Glen & Linda Ruiz, clients

"Anyone looking at Active Adult Communities should talk with Irene"

MJW, client

FOREWORD

Buying a new home can be a daunting task. It is one of the biggest financial decisions you will make in your lifetime. The anxiety of making such a large investment as you move into the retirement years creates even more intensity. You become overwhelmed by the multiple options of making your final "dream home" become a reality. Choosing the right realtor makes these decisions less stressful and more of an adventure.

Irene Hammond was our "adventure" leader. She was an expert in finding our "dream home" in a retirement community. She gathered information on our "wants" and "needs" and began looking at matches for our criteria. She knew the Active Adult Communities well, which helped us narrow our search. We appreciated her honesty and willingness to tell us if something that caught our eye would not be a good fit for us. This helped avoid mistakes we might have made on our own. This was particularly critical since we were moving from the Midwest to the Southwest. Even her "yes, no, maybe" answers were helpful in making decisions and narrowing our search. When our new home sales person commented, "She really knows her stuff" we were even more assured that Irene was keeping our best interests at the forefront. Her knowledge of resale and newly built homes was especially helpful. We looked at both options in our search. When we ended up buying a newly constructed home she was able to walk through the home and point out things we needed to have completed prior to signing off. We are grateful that we were able to access her expertise to find exactly what we wanted in a community as well as a new home.

Reading this book will allow you to learn from an expert. Best wishes as you join Irene on your adventure to find your dream home/community.

Mark and Linda Bettes

PREFACE

About a year ago, I heard someone speak about writing a book for your business. I thought "I could do that!" My husband, Rick, was encouraging and suggested I do it today and not put it off to someday. My mom, real-estate partner for years, Claudina said she would assist me and felt I should get going. One of my friends and fellow real estate associates, John Wake gave me an enthusiastic "I could totally see you doing that."

That is the story of how this dyslexic got started writing a book. Thank God for all the help I received from spell check, my mom, and my dear friend Deborah Dowe who lovingly did my first round of edits. Without them I don't know witch which is witch. So thank you for dotting my T's and crossing my I's.

I am very blessed, my family is alive, healthy and disease free. So when considering how I would pay it forward with my book, there wasn't any specific direction my life had been affected. I considered non-profits supporting seniors since this book is directed to a mature audience, none really pulled to me. Off in the other direction are children's charities. Rick and I have volunteered with the Boys and Girls Clubs of America several times and feel the children are our future. Giving as many children as possible the best opportunity to reach their full potential is always a win. A portion of the proceeds from this book's sales will be donated to the Boys and Girls Clubs of America.

Thank you for purchasing my book and for helping open the door to a great future for children across the country.

CONTENTS

Chapter 8
Real Estate

CHAPTER 1

WHAT IS AN ACTIVE ADULT COMMUNITY?

Not ready for the Old Folks Home! 50 feels like the new 30 but I'm all grown up and my kids are almost 30. I am not ready to retire! But I have earned the right to start to enjoy my life and do some of the things I have always wanted to do. How today does that happen? Welcome to the generation of the Active Adult Community, that creation of folks just like me who wanted more and got it! The early Boomers have perfected the lifestyle for the late boomers, Those who have just reached that magic age of 55 and have carved out locations from small condos on a beach to luxurious homes nestled in the mountains. They developed the concept and are just waiting for you to come along and enjoy it.

So what is an Active Adult Community?
The concept is that if you are at least 55 years old (or near it) you can use the Fair Housing Act* to live in a neighborhood with other adults and no kids. Oh your children and grandchildren can come and visit you, but only for a limited number of weeks a year. During those empty nest periods between visits you cure your boredom with rounds of golf, sets of tennis or pickle ball, if your knees are in need of a little gentler treatment. Maybe you want

to earn those master bridge points, or create an art masterpiece from glass or wood or gemstones. Want to cruise the islands? Or bike along a seashore, or join a motorcycle club to visit great lunch spots... during the week! It is all there, those early boomers have taken the kinks out and left the pleasure waiting for you.

The Fair Housing Act is a federal act in the United States intended to protect the buyer or renter of a dwelling from seller or landlord discrimination. Its primary prohibition makes it unlawful to refuse to sell, rent to, or negotiate with any person because of that person's inclusion in a protected class; race, color, religion, national origin, sex, disability, and familial status.

Familial status covers; families with children under the age of 18, pregnant women, and people securing custody of children under the age of 18.

The law within Fair Housing that allows for discrimination based on age is Housing for Older Persons Act (HOPA) there are two parts to the law, one is the 55 plus age community the other is a 62 year plus community. In the 62+ communities all residents must be a min of 62 years of age, (with the exception of caregivers) and most of these residences are care facilities. This is the strictest part of the HOPA act. The 55+ communities have an 80/20 allowance on the age requirement, and a few other less stringent requirements. The easiest way to demonstrate the ins and outs of this law are to answer a few questions that may directly apply to you.

The HOPA regulation states that the age census is counted by *residents*. Since residential property is most commonly acquired as owner occupied properties, proof of age must be provided with your purchase documentation.

Can live in a 55+ community if I am not yet 55?

Yes, No, Maybe. My clients hate when I answer a question that way, but it is the best answer...

Yes: The easiest way to purchase a home in a community when you are younger than the 55 age requirement is thru a builder. Builders are given a leniency on the census numbers while the community is being developed. From the point the community reaches 25% occupancy, the builder must maintain the age percentage parameters of a minimum of 80% of occupants having one person residing in the home being at least 55 year of age. The builder will enforce anyone purchasing into the community via resale to meet the mandatory age requirement; allowing the builder to have the flexibility to sell to the younger buyers while still maintaining the 80/20%

No: if you are interested in a resale home in a community where the builder is still present, they will only allow ownership to transfer via resale to owners that meet the 55 age minimum requirement. The builders are keeping a close watch on their census numbers - if you're 54, head over to the sales center.

Maybe: Since there is flexibility in the age of residents and 20% of residents can be younger than the 55 age minimum, many communities that are well within their census percentage are willing to allow for younger ownership. With HOA approval! You may see some communities/listings marketed as a 45+ or 50+ community. That isn't quite correct, they are a 55+ community allowing younger residents at the present time because their current census numbers are safely within the required HUD HOPA numbers.

My spouse is younger than I am, can they be on the deed as an owner?

Yes, is the answer to this one. Only one person in residence needs to be 55.

What if I die, can my younger spouse inherit the house and live in it?

Yes, is the answer to this one also, as long as that spouse is over 19. That 20% leeway given to the Homeowners Association by HOPA is for just this event.

Can my children inherit this home, and live in it?

Yes and No. Yes, they can own the property. They may choose to sell or lease it to an individual over 55.

HOPA does not prevent inheriting families from residing at the property even if they do have children under the age of 19. The Homeowner Association in their rules and regulations do have the power to discriminate against familial status and prohibit any families and children from residing in the community. If the HOA does allow for them to reside in the community the HOA has the right to restrict their use of community benefits.

Can my 20 something child live with me?

I hear this question often. Millennials are living at home longer and moving back after college, job layoffs, divorce... you name it. The magic age is 20. If they are 19 and younger they are considered children and not allowed to reside in your home for a period determined by the HOA, in my experience of 1-3 months. Find out about the clubhouse, they are going to be considered guests not residents, the HOA has the right to restrict the use of community benefits.

This rule restricting the duration of children visiting and residing in the community is one of the cardinal rules. One of my real estate instructors shared a story about a family here in Arizona. It was a tragic story of a boy whose parents died suddenly, and the only family he had were his grandparents. He was 19 and six months from his 20th birthday. The grandparents asked for special consideration to allow their grandson to live with them. The community would not grant them permission. They had 2 months to find a solution. The happy ending came because of the friendships the grandparents had in their community. A few of their friends offered to have the grandson live with them for a month or two, allowing him to live with no one household for longer than the community allowed. Once he was 20, he returned to his grandparents home… Happily ever after my favorite type of story!

How does anyone know my age?
When you purchase the property you must submit identification showing your age. The HOA is required to re-examine residents' identification periodically. Failing to do so risks loss of the Fair Housing Exemption and the property opening for residents of all ages.

Is an Active Adult Community right for me?
Do you like adventure, are you active, are you laid back, do you like new things, are you social, do you just want to get back to the things you love doing? What do you think you might like doing? Golf, fishing, tennis, pickle ball, cooking, wine tasting, motorcycle rides, lazy days by the pool…

Do as much or as little as you as you desire, the modern active adult communities have more in common with a cruise ship than the shuffleboard court, minus the waves and room service.

Active Adult Communities are big business. Pulte's Del Webb® division focuses exclusively on the Active Adult market, known for their branding of the Sun Cities. Currently in the greater Phoenix metro area we have the original Sun City, opened in the 1960's, and Sun City Grand, Sun City West, Sun City Festival, Sun City Anthem Merrill Ranch and Corta Bella. Shea homes has their Trilogy® branded Active Adult Living Communities, Lennar, AV Homes, and many other builders are in the very competitive market. The Baby Boomers have pushed the envelope and changed the face of the economy since they were born. Why should that change with retirement?

The early baby boomers have led the way, as they always have and created a whole new experience for those boomers on the latter half of the group. Builders and Developers are paying attention and asking lots of questions to find out exactly what you desire for today and into the future. Gone are the shuffle ball courts and welcome the new features: demonstration kitchens, pickle ball, travel clubs, spa's, yoga, concierge services and more.

No wheelchair races here, with cycle clubs, the motor kind and the bicycle too, these communities are not just about golf. They have evolved to include a diverse collection of interests and activities.

They have golf, in fact most of the golf courses built are in Active Adult Communities, after all who has the greatest free time to play, those of us who are retired. Being a golfer is not a requirement. In fact, most of my clients don't play golf. These communities are so much more.

What about my family and grandchildren? How close will I be able to be to them?
Many of the new communities are being incorporated within an all aged master planned community. Some share clubhouses, most

do have separate facilities. So your grandchildren and family could be just a few blocks away.

What types of homes are available?
Every option imaginable. Single family homes, single level and two stories, the two story homes are not as common but do exist. There are connected townhome or patio homes, condos even high rises. Some communities will offer several different property styles within its boundaries. If a community does offer different styles of properties, each grouping may have a different homeowners association fees. There may be a primary homeowner's association and a secondary association for properties with different service coverage.

CHAPTER 2

LIFESTYLE

These communities are all about lifestyle. If you are looking to have more friends, do more of the things you love, explore new skills, then an active adult community is the place for you.

What are the benefits of a large or a small community?
Each community has its own personality. Some you may like better than others. Finding the 'right' spot for you requires a little forethought. The community that is the best fit for you is going to depend on what you are looking forward to. Larger communities offer more clubs, activities and space for those clubs and groups to meet. Larger communities have multiple clubhouses, and facilities buildings. Some communities are so large they are truly like a city more than a neighborhood. The large communities do have advantages, the greater number of clubs allows for a more diverse collection of interests and possible activities to be involved with. A small community may have a sewing club, a large community will have several specific sewing clubs each with a different focus. A small community may have a jewelry /craft club, and the large community could have lapidary and silver smithing studios. The larger communities are more likely to have several different golf courses, and the players are grouped by handicaps rather than just men's and women's golfers.

Small communities offer the opportunity to get to know nearly everyone in the neighborhood. Each time you head to the clubhouse, you will see familiar friendly faces. In the larger communities, you may not know anyone when you walk in the clubhouse, unless you are participating at one of your club/ group gatherings. There are communities with Activities Directors on staff.

Are you looking for specific activities?

If the activities you are interested in require equipment and materials, metalworking or stained glass for example, a larger community is going to be a better fit. They are more likely to have the space for the club to meet and a greater resource for equipment to be acquired and enough people with the interest in the group to make it enjoyable for all involved.

If your interests only require a group of like minded people, maybe Bunko or Harley's; any sized community will be able to accommodate social meeting rooms to gather. The number of people who will be involved with depend on the size of the community. So if you move into a community and they don't have an Investment Club, you can start one!

Finding the sweet spot for you is the magic sauce. If you are into cycling, like my husband, you're not interested in a leisurely 5 mile ride like me. He is going to be looking for the group riding 40-100 miles each ride, and that takes a larger community, or being willing to look outside the community for additional clubs and social activities.

Why would I want a community with an Activities Director?

First thing an activity directors does is to assist homeowners in creating new interest groups as the community grows. Some activities directors will have a weekly welcome, what's happening in your neighborhood gathering. A great way to be introduced to a few other new residents and start getting involved. Since their job is to find out the interests of the community residents, they may already know several people interested in putting together an Automotive Restoration group or help you create a group for any other interest you may have. When a community has an activity director, there are more events happening that have nothing to do with one of the clubs. Super Bowl parties, sunset happy hour, pancake breakfast and more. Many times an activities director will set up a block of show tickets or sporting event with bus transportation to and from for your easy enjoyment, or something a bit farther away like an Alaskan cruise or a tour of Napa Valley with group pricing.

Why is there more than one pool in these active adult communities?

Many of the communities have more than one pool. If you are looking in a southern/ warmer climate most communities will have one outdoor resort pool designed for play, sunning, and relaxing. It may have a beach entry (no steps for easy access) attached spas, and plenty of lounging area. The second pool is for those people looking to swim laps, water aerobics and get some exercise. Many of the communities will have a separate lap pool, many times indoor so you can exercise year round. Other communities will incorporate the lap area as an extension of the resort pool. Water aerobics, water polo, water volleyball classes and groups also are held in the lap pool. The lap/exercise pool will either have a ramp entry with no steps and a handrail, or an electric chair hoist so everyone has access. No matter how young we feel, sometimes our bodies demand we take it a little easier. Beach entries may not be what you are looking for today in a community pool, you may be grateful for a ramp entry later.

I was looking forward to cruising and traveling, will I be alone?
One of the unique qualities of an active adult community is the ease in making new friends. Join the travel club or start one. If you don't have any desire to start a new group I am sure you will meet plenty of other people who would love to travel together. There are some communities with full time activities directors, and they may put together group trips for the whole community. There is bound to be a travel agent in the community somewhere who would be delighted to put a fabulous trip together. Maybe the Tennis Club puts a trip together to go see Wimbledon, or the Golfers have a trip put together to go play at Pebble Beach. Or your Dinner group heads to Napa together. So many options! Which ones will you choose?

I love baseball, is it true the active adult communities get busses and discount tickets?
Spring Training is a huge part of Arizona's winter and with 15 teams getting prepared for the baseball season in the Cactus League, baseball games have to be discussed. Realize you can insert any sport or sporting event, theater, concert, or event and the same will be true. If there is sufficient interest, YES a community will get group tickets, and arrange transportation if it makes sense to. Larger communities have activities directors that take care of all those details for you. Smaller communities will have to have someone take the reins and do all of the legwork themselves.

Can I bring my Harley?
Yes, and be sure to look for a home with extended garage or a garage that is extra wide for extra storage. Once you get settled in, be sure to connect with the Harley club and start enjoying the ride.

What do I do with my RV? Boat?
Most of the active adult communities are going to limit having your RV or boat parked in your front driveway. Each community

will set the timeframe for allowing boats and RVs to be in your front drive or street, in my experience it is 24-28 hours for the loading and unloading only. There are some communities that will have parking areas, for a fee, for boats and RV's, but that in my experience is not the norm. If a community does have RV and boat parking, it will be limited, and on first come first serve basis. So finding parking facilities, boat docks and other storage options will come from the surrounding area.

I really want to play golf every day, will I be able to afford it?
Check with each community you're considering and find out what their golf fees are. The cost for golf varies greatly, as you already know since you're a golfer. Also find out the size of the golf groups and their average handicaps. Golfing every day is a dream, but golfing with people who are at your level each day is even better.

How many golf courses can I play on?
Some golf courses offer reciprocal memberships. Some Active Adult Communities, have more than one golf course. Some communities are situated next to or close to another sister community with additional golf available. If golf is your passion, there are many options. Many times if the same builder (like Pulte Del Webb®) has built several communities in an area, you will be able to play on the neighboring communities golf courses at an adjusted resident rate.

Can I own my own golf cart?
A quick peak in the community parking lot will most likely let you know. Some communities are much more golf cart friendly. If the builder of the community had lots of homes with extended garages or the option to add an additional golf cart garage, you are likely to have more golf carts driving around. Some communities even have direct access to shopping, grocery stores and more via

golf cart. In many communities it becomes the preferred method of getting around, even if you don't play golf.

What about places of worship?

The larger communities may have places of worship within the community. In most cases you are going to have to drive outside of the community to find where you will go to worship. Since many of the communities are built a bit remotely, check on where you will have to drive to get to your place of worship. You will find a group of other friends who also go to the same place for services, carpool together, grab a bite to eat after, and even convoy together.

Is there a Tennis club?

Tennis, and now Pickle Ball are big favorites in many communities. How many tennis courts does a community have will give you an idea of how active the members are. Many of the larger communities have tournament courts great for spectator watching. Be sure to check out the gym for information on the tennis leagues.

If you are accustomed to the slower pace of clay and grass courts, you are not likely to find them in an Active Adult Community. The maintenance on clay and grass is just too high. You are more likely to find hard surfaced courts with different finishes.

What is Pickle Ball?

Pickle ball is a cross of tennis, badminton and ping pong. It sounds crazy... You play on a smaller court with a net similar to tennis. Rather than a racquet you use a paddle larger than a ping pong paddle. The ball is a plastic wiffle ball, making it move more slowly thru the air and similar to badminton.

Pickle Ball was invented just over 50 years ago on Bainbridge Island, Washington by a few families looking for something for the kids to do one summer day. The adults had so much fun playing, they kicked the kids off the court and kept playing themselves. Friends shared it with friends and now it is played across the country. The best part of the story is how it got its name. Pickles was the dog who was always stealing the ball.

CHAPTER 3

LOCATION, LOCATION, LOCATION

The three most important rules of real estate. For now, let's consider location in a bigger picture way. North, South, East, West - there are so many directions to go. As well as so many things to consider. You are not looking for a home near the best jobs, you are looking for your playground!

Where are your grandchildren and family?
The most common reason I hear about why someone is moving into or out of a community is Grand-babies. They are a huge draw. But realize, your kids and those luscious grand-babies, may not be staying in one spot long term. The workplace today is very different that it was even a decade ago. Be sure to consider if you want to chase your kids around from location to location and if financially it is even possible to do so! So if this move is a one and done, a stick and stay move, be sure to move to where YOU are going to be happiest. Not just where your kids and grandchildren are located at the time.

Do you expect to have the responsibility of caring for any grandchildren?

I always ask how close or how far away do you want to be from your family. If you want to have daily or regular babysitting duties then the closer the better. One of the master planned communities with a 55+ next door is perfect. If you want to be close enough to see your family and grand-babies regularly but not every day, a little farther away makes it subtly easier to not get together every weekend.

Where do your friends live?

Not going to follow your grandchildren. Then maybe you have friends in different areas you may consider. Many times if you are the first person who has found a great community and location, your friends will come visit, and fall in love with the community for themselves. This could start a domino of friends all moving to the same community or area. Many of the communities have state clubs. The Illinois club for example.

Is your spouse of the same mind?

So time for a conversation or two or three, about areas to consider. And if those grand-babies are in the mix for consideration, and you are considering locations that are _not_ close to them; take a look at how you are going to get to visit them. How often, and for how long? What is the drive time? And what type of roads will you have to travel on? Small winding roads, are beautiful to drive on a picture perfect day, they can be treacherous in storms or at night. Check out the distance of nearby airports and flights to your family. What airlines are flying in and out of that airport? It may be time to get a new rewards credit card. What are the direct flights out of that airport, are those direct flights to the cities you need to get to? Living in a quiet area, that is a long drive to an airport, and no direct flights to the kids, may be misery for traveling and your wallet.

The next big consideration is **What have you envisioned for your retirement?** Your big picture may be all about golf, or travel, or... it's your vision, fill in the blank!

In what part of the country have you envisioned your retirement? I have been blessed to never really have to shovel snow. If you haven't' been that lucky, that may be one of the items you are looking to eliminate from your retirement life. You're not alone, that is why the majority of Active Adult Communities are located in southern states. The majority but not all!

Retirement offers the opportunity to be outside, enjoying the activities you never had time for while working. With retirement comes the desire to take advantage, year round of the things you love to do.

Do you plan on creating a home base and traveling a lot?
In that case a community closer to a major airport. You may make a friends with someone willing to do airport runs in your community. I know I hate 5am airport runs, so since many of the communities are to the outskirts of the city, find out if is Uber friendly, or if Super Shuttle services are available?

What about the cost of living?
Be sure to research the cost of living for areas you're considering. There are really big differences in property taxes state to state! If you're accustomed to your property taxes being equivalent to a second mortgage, the financial freedom of a lower property tax state could give you a very different lifestyle. Some states have state income tax, an expense that you may not have considered

when choosing a location. CYA (Call your Accountant) to find out how state taxes may impact your bottom line.

How long are you planning on living in this house?

Are you planning on staying in this community and location for just a few years, or long term. If you are just going to be here for a few years, consider the resale market of community. If you are considering two communities ask your Realtor® what the average number of "Days on Market" is for a resale home in each community and ask them why the difference, if any. Understanding that *market conditions change!* and today's market may be very different than when you go to sell. The reasons one community sells faster than another could hold true in a different market as well.

If you purchase a home in a new community and have your home built. When will the builder be complete in the community? If you are competing against a builder when it is time to sell. Understand that no matter how many upgrades you put in, your home will only sell for less than what the builder is asking for a home with similar upgrades. The next buyers are going to consider their options for resale or picking and designing their new dream home. Your house will have to be attractively priced to compete. Sometimes a builder will retire a floor plan. This can be a good thing for you, if you have the retired floor plan your home is now no longer available for a buyer to purchase through the builder and if it is a fabulous layout you are in luck, it's like you are not competing with the builder quite as much and can be a little stronger in your pricing.

What are your hobbies or favorite activities?

Do you love history? Then an area near our country's capital or founding colonies could be a great location. Golf? Then head to warmer climates where you can golf all year round. Boating? Fishing? Hiking? Pick a location that will have the easiest access to the activities you love.

How is your health?
Doctors used to tell people with allergies to head to the desert. Well the desert is all planted up and I am here to let you know people have allergies in the desert too. The advantage to moving to a different climate is you haven't had a chance to develop allergies to the area foliage. If you are allergic to citrus trees (that's a big one) Florida, Arizona and California are going to be misery in March. If you can take a cruise for the month you're all set otherwise plan on a date with your pharmacist.

How do you respond to humidity, or desert, or altitude?
Well I am here to let you know that all warmth is not created equal. I have lived in Florida and Arizona, I personally love the dry heat of the Southwest over the humidity of the Southeast. Before you pick one over the other, visit both and find out what feels best to you! You may be surprised.

Altitude affects your heart and blood pressure. Specifically the oxygen saturation of your blood. The good news, the longer you live at elevation the stronger your body becomes. That is why so many athletes train at altitude. It is also why the Denver Broncos have a true home field advantage. However moving to altitude when you already have health issues may not be the smartest choice. Check with your doctor and again, visit and see how you feel. When a walk down the street has you out of breath, and climbing a flight of stairs is work... it isn't the right place to live.

CHAPTER 4

SECURITY FINANCIAL AND PHYSICAL

A new community most likely means a new city and state too. You have questions, ask them. I tell my clients, no question is too small. What kind of security is in the community? What if I only choose to live there seasonally? What do I do with my home? How easy is it for me to try new things in the community? Your Realtor® is a fabulous information resource.

When I think of Security it is not only my personal well being and my belongings, but my financial security as well. Understanding the costs of living in one of these communities and how that will affect your budget and lifestyle.

I haven't purchased a home in 20 years, what expenses can I expect beyond the actual purchase price?
Closing costs are going to vary state to state. They vary greatly when you look at the differences of a cash purchase to purchasing with a home loan. First let me disclose that I am not familiar with the differences of closing in a state where lawyers are required. I can only assume that the fees may be higher. Cash purchases can expect to have 1-2% in closing costs. When purchasing a home

with a loan, you can anticipate 5-7% closing costs as a rough estimate. One item that can increase these closing cost numbers is the homeowners association fees. Many communities have larger fees for homeowners when they first acquire a property. (also see in Chapter 8 What are my purchasing options?)

What regular monthly bills can I expect to have?

Generally you can expect to have the same bills you currently have. Electric, Water, Cable, Phone. If the home you select is a free standing single family home, you will also most likely have all of the home maintenance, like roof repair, ac/heat, landscaping. Check with your Realtor® to confirm the expenses and maintenance that you will be required to take care of.

You will have either a Homeowners Association or a Recreation Membership with any of the Active Adult Communities. Association fees have a broad range depending on the size and services made available to the community.

Are there any fees I should know about in an Active Adult Community?

Yes, These communities will have either Homeowners Association (HOA) fees, or Recreational Community fees. Depending on the community and how often they collect monthly/quarterly/annually and what the fees are you will need to pay your HOA or Recreation fees in <u>advance</u> for a min of 3 months at your closing. They will be prorated to your closing date. Most of the communities also have a few additional fees, mainly paperwork fees most commonly called Transfer Fees or Disclosure Fees. These are usually a $100-$400. If there are any current assessments, they must be disclosed and either the buyer or seller will pay depending on terms agreed to in the contract.

The largest of the fees normally is the Capital Improvement Fee. Sometimes called asset preservation, capital reserve, community enhancement or future improvement fees. I feel it is an important, relevant and worthwhile fee. (really!) It is charged to EVERY buyer as they purchase into the community. The money goes directly to the HOA bank account to use as needs arise or are planned for. Painting the Clubhouse, new computers for the computer lab, resurfacing the pool, new chairs in the Clubhouse, are examples. It helps keep the community resources up to date without needing to do assessments. See I told you it was worthwhile. The constant influx of funds allows the HOA Board to update, improve, expand and beautify your new community. This onetime fee many times is calculated by a multiplier of monthly HOA fees, 6 or 8 months for example. Or a flat fee.

Homeowners fees don't always stay the same. If expenses rise, HOA fees can also rise. If large expenses have not been accounted for, the home owners association may do a special assessment to every owner to cover these costs. The capital improvement fee is designed to help offset the community needing to do special assessments, but they still may come. If you have concerns or issues about how your homeowners association is allocating funds, get involved and join your Board of Directors, come to your HOA Meetings, and be part of the solution.

What kind of security is there in these communities?
Most of the communities are designed with limited ingress/egress. A limited number of access roads in and out of the community discourage random traffic through the neighborhood. This design plan is perfect for creating a more secure community.

There are also gated, and guarded communities. A gated community will have a gate with a code, usually smaller communities are more likely to use an unmanned gate with a call box so anyone can call a resident to have them open the gate and access the community. These communities will have a second resident only gate as well. All of the unmanned gates are accessible with a resident clicker or swipe card.

Larger communities have too much traffic to allow for an unmanned gate. So if a larger community is gated the main access gate will be guarded. Having a guarded community, is an indication that it usually will also have a higher homeowner's fee. The residents must pay for not only the maintenance and electric use of the gate but also the salaries of the people working at the guard house. Many times, residents from the community may be hired on to work part time at the guard house.

Some communities, gated or un-gated, have security services drive thru looking for any suspicious activity, or more general monitoring, like water flowing out the garage, indicating a leaking hot water heater, reporting back to the HOA so they can let you know.

What do I do when I want to go away for a month? Or longer?
Many or even most people who live in Active Adult Communities do not live there 365 days a year. Visiting family, vacation, second homes, a cruise or a road trip... everyone gets out of town sometime. Most communities, once you get to know your neighbors, will have someone who either as a favor or for a side income, oversees properties. Choose someone who passes by your home every day when they take their walk. That way, if there have been fliers or newspapers left on your doorstep, they can gather them up. Once every couple of weeks, they can go into your home, flush the toilets, run water in the sinks to fill the p-traps, and make sure your home is safe and sound. With today's technology, you can control lights, your heating and air conditioning and more from your smart phone. With affordable

motion sensored cameras that email or text you and take high definition video, knowing your house and belongings are safe is simple.

Remember, most of your neighbors are also already retired. That means homes are not sitting empty and alone all day while you're at work. Neighborhood watches don't need to be set up by the police. They just occur naturally.

One more strange thing… it may only be in Arizona, I am not sure. We do have several communities that the post office will not hold mail while you are away on vacation. There are too many 55+ communities in the area and the post office simply doesn't have the space to accommodate everyone. In these communities, the incoming mail boxes are designed to have the bottom removed and a container (deeper than your arm) installed below so the mail can drop to the bottom. Then it is accessed from the back side at the bottom with a key. I told you it was strange. It works!

I am disabled, are the community center and activities accessible to me?
All of the community center buildings are public buildings and fall into the same building codes for all public spaces. For wheelchair access, most communities have push button opening doors. Ramps where needed and elevator access.

Can I have the house I buy configured for a wheelchair?
This is where I emphasize not all builders that are building 55+ communities are designing equally. One of the goals of living in an Active Adult Community is to have the ability to 'age in place'. It is a new buzzword that means I like where I live and I choose to stay and live in my home as long as possible! One of elements builders need to be conscious of as they build in the adult communities is

'aging in place'. Not all do. Pay attention to design elements that may make it harder to accommodate wheelchair access later. Are the hallways wide and open? Would you have to navigate sharp corners to access bedrooms and bathrooms? Is the kitchen built with minimum space between cabinets? Are there any interior steps in the house? How many steps to get into the home. Is there an option for a zero grade (no steps) into the home? Is the shower accessible for a walker or wheelchair?

A builder has to accommodate for anyone with disabilities to access and use their home. Americans with Disabilities Act and the Fair Housing Act both are on your side here. This includes lowering counter tops, light switches, ramp access, shower and bathroom modifications. Some may come with an extra charge as a modification, and any and all can be added to a new construction home.

In a resale home, the seller does not have to make any alterations for you. You will need to make those once you acquire the home. In addition to the items I have already mentioned, look at the shower and if it will have to be reconfigured for access. Grab rails are easy to install, even making adjustments to door frames can be relatively simple with a good contractor.

Will I be a big fish in a little pond, or a little fish in a big pond in an Active Adult Community?
Feeling comfortable in any situation especially when making new friends is important. One of the reasons for visiting a community prior to purchasing it is to get a feel for the people in the community. You don't want to find yourself in a community that really revolves around golf if you don't play. If you love to travel the world and are able to do so, you want a community that also has residents that financially can do the same, and maybe join you. Many times you can get a feel if a community is going to be

a good fit by driving thru, talking to a few residents and looking at their monthly/ quarterly newsletter and activity guide. It is not just about finding a community with the activities you enjoy, but also finding a community where the residents are financially in the same relative income bracket, allowing for you to feel comfortable throughout your community. Every community isn't the right fit for everyone. Find the right fit for you! And your fish pond will be a delight to swim in.

Do I pay for each activity I use at the center? Which come free?
Check with the community you are considering! Most activities are going to be included in your HOA or Recreation fees. Some clubs may have a small social fee, this is to offset the cost for parties and gatherings. Or a 'key' fee, since different clubs have either storage closets, or specific rooms they meet in, a key is made for members of the club. Some clubs may have a min fee for materials; if the group purchases a specific amount of materials they can get a discount. Group buying. If there is a teacher or trainer, for example a yoga instructor for your yoga class, there may be a fee for the class so the instructor is paid. Rarely have I ever found a community have a fee to use any of the meeting rooms. So any additional fees are utilized by the members or participants of the group.

So if you are wondering if the activities you like best could have additional fees, first consider the cost of that activity if you were to do it outside of the community, does it make sense that the club would charge a little to give you better value? A Bunko group may charge $10 a year social fee, and the fee covers food at their annual party. Where the silversmithing club will have fees for equipment use, maintenance and replacement and bulk purchase of silver to save all the members on their creations.

Is there a Gym membership?

Yes, No, Maybe… here I go again. Ask in the community you are considering. Some of the communities do have gym fees, many times the fees can be covered by the Silver Sneakers program available with most senior health plans. This offsets the costs of new equipment, and staffing of trainers in many communities. In other communities there are no fees for access to the gym, only fees for classes or having a trainer work with you. The fees are normally very reasonable since your homeowners or recreation fees cover the cost of the facility, you are only paying for the time of the class teacher or trainer.

Can I use my golf cart on the streets?

Most residential community streets are 35 miles per hour or less, and golf carts can travel on them. Many times the perimeter roads around an active adult community are over the 35mph max. In that case you can cross the street but not travel on the street.

Golf carts are not just for golfers!

Some communities are super golf cart friendly. They are a great way to get around the neighborhood, access the clubhouse and visit friends. Some communities even have grocery store access, and you never have to get on a main road.

How do you know if the community you are considering is golf cart friendly? At the clubhouse, are there more parking areas for golf carts than cars? Do you see everyone buzzing around on their golf carts? Do homes for sale have golf cart garages, or larger garages to accommodate a golf cart? Find out if you can access any retail shopping via golf cart as well.

Can I store my RV in the community?

Sometimes. Most communities don't have the space available for you to have an RV garage connected to your home. They are more likely to have golf cart garage connected instead. Some communities will have an optional storage lot for RV parking. First come first serve, and there will most likely be an additional fee for usage of the space. Check the surrounding area for RV storage options if the community doesn't have any available on site.

Most associations will have restrictions on the parking of an RV in front of your home. It may only be allowed for 24-48 hours, just for the purpose of loading and unloading.

Will I have to pay school taxes with my property taxes?

There are a few communities that have been laid out prior to school districts being established, and with no children permitted within the community, there are no school district taxes collected. This keeps the property taxes low in those communities. The majority of communities however are in a school district making no tax benefit for residing in an Active Adult Community.

CHAPTER 5

ALTERNATIVES – NON 55

You like the idea of an Active Adult Community but are not quite sure if it is the right fit for you. **What other options are out there?** And what should you consider when choosing a community that is not age restrictive?

Maybe the Active Adult Communities are not in the area you are considering to move, or maybe you feel you're just 'too young' to be in one of 'those' communities, or the community doesn't feel right for you. Whatever the reason, it's all good. There are lots of master planned communities and country club communities out there. First let me give you my description of each.

A Master Planned Community is one where there are several types of housing. Many times, but not always, built by several different builders, with schools and parks designed into the community, some of these communities will have clubhouses, with pools and activity rooms. If they have a clubhouse they will most likely have many, many different activities available. Fees many times will be just Homeowners Association fee or standard maintenance fees. Additional fees associated with services that require paying a person to perform or lead that service. For example, access and use of the gym is part of the HOA, but exercise classes with an instructor have an added fee.

A Country Club Community will be very similar to the master planned with a Homeowners Association but to have access to the facilities requires a separate membership fee and possibly a buy in. There may be several levels of membership with different degrees of access to facilities. Many times Golf is an additional membership over the Social Membership.

The last example is what I refer to as a **House on the Street** this is a home in a community that does not have any facilities, clubhouses or easy connection points to meet, mingle and socialize with neighbors.

What are the differences between the communities?
The big obvious difference of an all aged Master Planned or Country Club community compared to an Active Adult Community is the diversity of ages. That factor can be considered an asset or a hindrance.

Let me explain, and compare:

At the pool, in the Active Adult Community there are specific hours when kids or grandchildren are allowed at the pool. Separating quiet hours and noisy hours. Whereas in a multi-generational community children can be playing at the pool anytime.

CHAPTER 6

HEALTH CARE

I have to admit, we aren't 20 anymore, and health care needs to be an important part of the decision. Moving forward from where you are, diagnostic services and ongoing medical care are both to be considered.

Take into consideration not only your current heath issues if any, but also what conditions are you at higher risk for? How far will you have to travel to get to doctors? Specialists? Hospitals? Emergency services? If the community you are considering is farther away from medical services what are the drive times? If you need ambulance service, from where will emergency vehicles be driving?

I know you don't want to think about getting sick and needing medical assistance. Over time, especially if you plan on living in this community and in this house long term, at some point even if it is only for annual checkups, you are going to need medical services.

Make a call to your health insurance provider. Find out if the areas available services are in your coverage plan. What adjustments will you need to make to have the full healthcare coverage in the area you are considering.

Get on your health insurance provider's website and check out the doctors in the area. Are they accepting new patients? It's not enough for Doctors to be in the area, they also need to be available for you to become their new patient. Transferring records is simple these days. Once you setup your first appointments, have the doctor's office send over the authorization form with all the contact info on your old physicians and let the doctor's office do the rest. One great advantage of technology. Check out the doctors reviews too, websites like Vitals.com and HealthGrades.com allow patients to let you know how they like their Doctors.

Accept the fact that the newest communities with the newest amenities are built on the outlying areas of larger cities and that medical facilities may not have yet been built within reach. That is great today while your healthy as an ox, but not so if you are in need of those services. Find out when medical services are expected to be built and provided in the area. Are there already plans to built a hospital? Or just a clinic? Over time, the health care amenities are going to be built, and there will be more available. New community builders have a *'build it and they will come'* perspective. Yes, as the people come, so do the amenities, but there has to be enough people to warrant the cost of a new facility.

Whether you may find yourself dealing with high blood pressure, osteoporosis, or other medical issues, the study of medical gerontology and specialists in geriatrics start to become more important because of their specialized knowledge in the area of our aging bodies. If the neighboring hospital is known for their maternity ward, make sure they also have sufficient staffing and specialists in the geriatric fields. Geriatrics isn't a bad word, it simply defines the branch of medicine dealing with the care of aging adults. If the community is still new, the "build it and they will come" philosophy will eventually bring qualified specialists to the medical facilities in the surrounding area.

The term *geriatrics* comes from the Greek *geron* meaning "old man", and *iatros* meaning "healer".

Mayo Clinic, Cleveland Clinic and MD Anderson are three of the top diagnostic facilities in the country. They have facilities in Arizona, Florida, Texas, Nevada, Minnesota, Ohio and New Jersey. It's not surprising that the alternate campuses of each of these big medical companies all have mild winters and are popular retirement and Active Adult Community locations.

CHAPTER 7

RELATIONSHIPS

Everyone, when moving to a new place wants to be confident that they can make friends. When we were kids, we made our friends in school. As young adults we connected with our workmates and people from our interest groups and church or synagogue. As we married and had families of our own, our friendships came through our children's interests. With the kids gone and out of the house, and in retirement our workplace isn't a source of new friends. How do you go about staying social and active?

If you're not considering moving to an Active Adult Community, you can check out your city's continuing education program or area universities for classes and learning programs to keep body and mind active. You could find social groups on meetup. com, where their motto is "What do you love?" they offer the opportunity to connect with groups that do darn near anything you can imagine, hobbies, and fitness, to dinner clubs, hiking groups and more are all available. Looking to stay close to home? Check out NextDoor.com a private neighborhood only way to connect, socialize and find someone to repair the kitchen sink. Another great resource for connecting with others is to volunteer.

If you are not going to be moving to an Active Adult Community you are going to have to work a little harder at staying active and social. There are plenty of places you can connect wherever you live, some communities just make it simple.

Now, you are considering an Active Adult Community. Visit it! Grab the activity schedule. Smaller communities will have fliers, and larger communities will have a newsletter/magazine. Check out all of the clubs, what looks interesting to you? There is almost always a contact person listed for each group. Give a call to the contact person for the group or club you know you want to be apart of. Have a chat... arrange for a coffee or lunch or to join the group while you're in town visiting. What better way to already establish a relationship, or several before you even move in!

One of the most common reasons for choosing a specific location is family relationships; Primarily Grandchildren! Grandchildren may be the impetus to bring you to an area, but the relationships you will make while living in the community will make truly love where you live.

One of the unique things about the active adult communities, is that everyone has been the new kid on the block. And if you build a home, then you are all the newbies on your block. What this does is put everyone on the same page for making new friends. It is a truly unique situation, and creates an open door and welcoming culture you may have never experienced before.

You're making friends thru your interests. (be sure to read the chapter on lifestyle) When your social circle revolves around your interests and not soccer practice and piano lessons, you know *Retirement isn't Boring.*

I'm widowed or divorced is it easy for me to make friends too?
Yes! Many communities have Ladies and Gentlemen's clubs. These clubs are not limited to just those who are single, rather limited by gender because we all know *Men are from Mars and Women are from Venus* and we socialize differently. If you are single, looking to date, or stay single, larger communities will offer a greater selection of social groups specifically geared toward the singles in the community.

I don't drive? Can I get around?
That is another Yes, No, Maybe answer. The larger communities and many times the more established communities offer more services, some offer volunteers who bring people to medical appointments, other communities have van services like a community public transportation, there may be pick up and drop off at area stores and medical offices as well.

Many of the communities have grocery stores and some shopping accessible from the community with just a golf cart. You will need to check the state laws on driving golf carts on the streets and if a driver's license is a requirement. With more electric vehicles on our roads the laws are changing.

LGBT Communities
Our world has become more inclusive to everyone. There are a few specifically LGBT Active Adult Communities around the country and even a few assisted living communities as well. Many of the communities are specifically women only, others are women and men.

The Realtor® in me must pipe in here... Protected classes are identified to keep homes and communities from discriminating against people. The Protected classes identified by the Fair

43

Housing Act are: race, color, religion or creed, national origin, sex, disability and family status.

Sexual orientation is not yet a protected class, and these communities can not limit the people by their sexual orientation who live in the communities. Sex (male or female) is a protected class but these communities cannot discriminate based on sex. The only caveat to the Fair Housing Act permitting discrimination is the Housing for Older Persons Act. (see chapter 1 for more info)

Many of these communities are not age restrictive, so anyone may choose to purchase within them. The communities have focused their marketing to the LGBT community and the communities have become known for the sexual orientation of the majority of the residence.

If one of the LGBT communities is not a good fit for you for whatever reason, I suggest a larger active adult community. Within a larger community you will find a greater diversity and a larger number of like minded people.

Families are all about Holidays
Holiday traditions may be changing. With a new home, and new community, you may choose to do something different for your family celebrations. Depending on the proximity to your family members, ease of travel for everyone: This may be the opportunity to pass the torch to the next generation for hosting those big gatherings with all the generations present. Hand down the turkey platters and baking pans for your children to start doing all the food preparation and hosting.

No, that's not an option. How could I even consider it! Find me a house with a big kitchen and dining room to sit the whole gang! Or maybe not! Don't worry many communities will have options.

Some communities will have full kitchens that you can reserve for events, other communities will have catering options with banquet halls you can reserve on property. Most communities have rooms that can be adjusted to accommodate different sized gatherings. Just like hotel banquet centers. If having the whole gang over to your home is a must, check out what the activities center has available and what their policies are for reserving over the busy season.

Religion

Many of us have created deep bonds with the friends and community we have had in Church or Synagogue. That continues in an Active Adult Community. You will need to verify the distance of your desired place of worship. Some communities have worship sites within the community. Most you will have to travel outside of the community to attend services. Churches and Synagogues and any other worship sites offer wonderful ways to get involved with your town and community outside of the Active Adult Community gates.

CHAPTER 8

REAL ESTATE

The first rule of Real Estate is Location, Location, Location! That is always true. Finding the right location for you is the first importance.

Many people are launching out into new interests and careers, if that is you, the location needs to be 'work friendly' close to the required resources for your endeavors. Maybe working from home is a big component, and having a home office space, with high speed technology services are a must. The high speed technology is a must in any situation if you ask me! Or maybe you still choose to work part time, are there places for you close! Finding a community within reasonable distance to businesses, commerce and resources is going to be key.

The magic word in the last sentence is *reasonable*. Many of the Active Adult Communities require large parcels of land and are built further away from most stores, hospitals and commerce. Communities that are in the early stages of development more noticeably so than communities that have been building and established for years. Build it and they will come is true, build the community, and other businesses will pop up around as the population grows and the demand is present.

Now that we have narrowed down to a community or two... what about the house. This is where you Realtor® is a huge support. Each area is a bit different; in Arizona our hot sun is always a consideration. The main living areas are normally to the back of the home, so the west setting sun super desirability in winter months is miserable in the summer. So if you are intending to reside in the home year round, a west backyard is not going to be your first choice. In areas with snowfall the front of the house facing south is always a plus, less ice and quicker snow melt! If you're moving to a new climate, be sure to ask your agent what items should you be aware of in picking your new home.

New communities, as I have mentioned previously, require a large parcel of land to support all of the amenities. If you fall in love with a lot that has amazing views, double check what is going to be built in the area, if the land beyond your lot isn't owned by the builder, realize it could become ANYTHING!

Location still is important as you choose the lot if you are going to purchase a new construction home, Look at the ingress and egress to the community, do you want to be right at the busy entrance? Think about 10 years down the road, will that road be a major highway as growth progresses closer to the borders of your community? Do you really want to be able to walk to the clubhouse or might you prefer to be a short golf cart ride away? Lots of things to take into account besides the actual dimensions of the land.

What is a stay and play? This is when a builder invites you to stay on the property and sample the facilities and wander through the model homes. It usually includes a round of golf, maybe a treat from their spa, use of the tennis courts, pools and an intro to the various special activities available. It might include a dinner with a few of the residents so you can quiz the actual homeowners instead of a salesperson. These visits are not free, but are quite reasonable for the amenities included. The goal of course, is for you to fall in love and buy a home from the builder.

Your Realtor® will pleased to be able to arrange these visits for you. In fact if you do not let us arrange the stay, we are not permitted to take part in the purchase of your home with you. Most builders require that if you are going to use the services of a Realtor® that the Realtor® must accompany you on your first visit.

Reservations during the high season of an area may be needed several months in advance. If it is off season, the community may have availability with only a few days notice.

If there are several new construction communities in an area, you may be able to string a few stays together and get a sampling of several communities.

When is best to visit?
That depends on when you plan on living in the community. If you are going to reside in this home just during the high season; definitely visit during the high season. That is when you are going to live in the community after all. If you are going to be a year round resident, visit during the off season. Some communities are still bustling with activity even in the off season, and others are limited in activities and people.

What to look for while visiting?
Check out the activity guide, what is going on in the community,

If the clubhouse is packed with people, and the community is only ¾ built, it could be an indication that the facilities are not able to support the community. By the same token, understand that a community still in it's construction phase will be adding people, so a quiet community center may simply be an indication of a young community with growing room.

The size and location of a community will create a very different experience.

Small communities are going to feel like being in a small town "everyone knows your name" or was that a neighborhood bar? Either way you know what I mean. Meanwhile you can get lost in a big community. Where you have your friends and the people you, let's say, play tennis with, and you do all kinds of things together, but you don't know the group that plays softball. There can be a huge difference in what activities and groups are available in a small community vs a larger one. Sun City West in Arizona, one of the largest Active Adult Communities, has over 30,000 residents, over 100 different active clubs, 4 Clubhouses, 7 golf courses and so much more. It really is a city!

Should I purchase a new build or purchase resale?
That is really going to depend on your personal budget and taste. If you look at the resale homes and think of remodeling, definitely head to the sales office and have it done to your taste and style the first time! If you are not particular about the finishing in a home, and you don't have a great desire for a brand new home, then resell could be just the right direction to choose.

What are the pros and cons of buying a new construction home?
Once you close on your new construction home expect to have a little more work and money invested to really be ready to live in your new house. Paint, blinds, ceiling fans and other items may be needed.

Options, options and more options. Both a pro and a con. Once you decide to build your home the options and choices may seem endless. Relax, the design center decorators are there to assist you, they know their inventory and will work with you to stay in your budget. Realize they have to let you know of every option; you don't have to get them all.

Landscaping may or may not be included in the final home, it is possible that just the front yard is landscaped by the builder prior to closing, and the back yard is needing to be completed. Usually by this time you would have already been in touch with landscapers to complete the job. The builder usually has one or two companies they can suggest, or drive around the newly completed neighborhoods and look for landscaping signs, or stop and have a chat with your new neighbors and ask who they used and if they like the work that was done. Landscapers working in the area are familiar with the Home Owner Association requirements for landscaping, and you can easily view their completed work. Be aware, many times there is a timeframe for landscaping to be completed, making it a do sooner rather than later task.

Window Treatments. The builders don't normally have a great selection of window treatments, they just are not in that business. Custom made plantations shutters is one exception. Since the builder uses the same sizes of windows thru all their homes and communities, mass producing custom made shutters creates a better value, in my experience, than waiting and doing it later. If you don't opt for the plantation shutters, plan on having window treatments at the top of your to do once you move in.

You are likely to still have some construction around your home. This will include early morning workers, the sound of hammers, trucks and more. Lots of extra vehicles during the day on the streets. Be patient, most builders build one neighborhood before moving on to the next. The custom built communities will sell the lots, and build one house here then one over there. The

Production builders will sell all the lots in an area, or close to it before moving on. Production builders will also build a spec home on lots that did not get grabbed up, so they can have their crews move on the next area together.

One of the best parts of moving into a brand new home, whether you build from scratch or choose a spec home, is all the neighbors are moving in at the same time. Neighborhood gatherings, get to know you soirees are the norm. Since everyone is the "new kid on the block."

Which offers a better value, building a house with the builder or purchase a resale home?
Most of the time, you are going to find the best final price in a community in the resale market. All of the "moving in" finishes are complete, you don't have to worry about window treatments, landscaping etc… Most of the time homes available in the resale market are a few years old and most of the warranties are no longer valid. Be sure to have a home inspection! And ask the seller for a home warranty service coverage for the first year. That way you have a service plan if something does fail.

Another great value is a Spec Home, a home built on speculation that someone will want a new home without having to wait the full build time before they move in. The Speculation homes, or Spec homes, have already had all of the options chosen. If it has just been started then just the framing options and electrical extras have been chosen. Then, at the required timeframe, their designers have gone thru and selected interior finishes, counter tops, flooring and all of the other extras. In most cases, you don't have any options waiting to be selected. The closer the Spec home is to completion the more the builders want to get it off their books and get it sold. It is the only time the builders are negotiable in my experience! So ask for the appliance package (washer /dryer/ fridge) to be added in, or a few thousand more for closing costs. The builders already discount these homes so they may not agree, but it is always worth asking. This is going to be the best value you will receive and have a newly built home, with all of the warranties.

Walking thru the builder's models is similar to walking thru a home in Architectural Digest. Beautifully designed, decorated and styled. The finishes may be the highest end of offerings from their design center, and many times there are design features (wainscoting as one) that the builder does not have available. If you love a design item, ask the salesperson from the builder's site for availability and cost. I see many builders show their models with lovely window upgrades, bay windows, rolling walls of glass, oversized sliders, etc, be sure to find out what the standard is on the home model that you are considering. Ask to see a Spec Home or one in the community that is almost complete with construction. Or ask your Realtor® to show you that floor plan in the community so you can see "realistically" how that home will look once complete.

Is it possible to buy the Model?
Yes, sometimes. Some of the builders will offer their model homes for sale and rent them back while they are selling that floor plan. The rental timeframe can be a couple of years or until they complete the community, sometimes that can be quite a while. The advantages: you may get a highly upgraded home, upgraded landscaping, pools etc, Many times the lot the home sits on is highly desirable. The lot may come with the best views in the community, or water feature on the golf course, or close to the clubhouse... and if you can wait the few years before moving in, it could be a dream home in the perfect location. The disadvantage is, the home has had a ton of people walk thru, so ask about the condition of the carpeting when the builder finally hands over the home to you. The home has also sat for some time frame without

any water going thru the pipes causing dry fittings. A friend of mine worked customer service for a builder, and a common issue she received was pipe and water damage from the previous model homes. Confirm the warranty you will receive after you take possession of the home!

Buying a home from the builder do I need a Realtor®?
I am a Realtor®, I feel that the purchase of a home regardless of if you purchase a resale, or from a builder, you should have representation. So YES, you should have a Realtor® represent you when you purchase a new construction home.

Does using a Realtor® affect the price I pay for my home?
No, The builder offers compensation to your agent if they are with you when you first visit the new build community. When you arrive, the builder's sales agent will ask you to sign in with your Realtor®. The registration documentation from the builder will declare the amount of compensation they pay Realtor®s. The caveat to this is: If you have a buyer broker agreement for a different amount of compensation refer to your buyer broker agreement for how the difference is compensated for.

The builder and the builders agent represent the interests of the builder. Not you! The builder's contract is *not* the standard state residential real estate purchase contract, it is the builder's contract and it is written in the interest of the builder, not you the buyer. Having a Realtor® who is knowledgeable about the builders contracts and what you the buyer need to be aware of is important. The builder has specific time frames for actions to be completed. Working with their lender, or providing the needed documentation if paying cash, making design center appointments, walkthroughs and more.

In Arizona, where I live, the most important document you sign as part of their contract is that you have READ the Public Report. Not that you have received it but that you read it. I rarely have had a builder's sales agent hand over the Public Report and ask the buyers to read it. But everyone has you sign that you have. The public report is the only disclosure document that the seller (builder) provides. What was this land before it was this community. Where is the nearest airport, is this a flood zone, is there a freeway coming in next to the homes, do you have fire services, etc. It is the document that lets you know what is in the area to be concerned with. I ask the sales agent to hand that over so you the buyer can review it while the builders agent gets their paperwork together.

What Realtor® should I choose?
Any chapter on real estate in a book about Active Adult Communities, would not be complete without talking about the Senior Real Estate Specialist Designation (SRES) by the National Association of Realtor®s. The National Association of Realtor®s (NAR) is America's largest trade association, one aspect of NAR is education. Currently there are 26 different designations where a Realtor® can increase their knowledge and skills in a specific area. One of these designations is SRES. SRES specifically addresses the needs of the 50+ buyers and sellers. The designations requires 2 days of classroom study, or equivalent online coursework.

I have also created a directory of agents who are knowledgeable and familiar with the Active Adult Communities in their areas. I have spoke with each of them and they are excited to assist you in finding the best community and home for your next chapter!

Show me the money... What are your purchasing options?
The first options is **Cash**. A large percent of people retiring want to reduce their monthly outgoing funds, and any financial advisor will let you know, your mortgage is one of if not the largest expense you have monthly. Eliminating your monthly mortgage payment reduces what you need to have coming in each month for your retirement. Even though homeowners were hard hit in 2006-2008 home values have moved back upward and in many areas back to where home prices were in 2005 before the bust, some areas are even higher. Cashing out on the equity in your current home, and purchasing a new home with cash, may require downsizing a bit, but getting rid of the monthly payment is a godsend.

I am not sure if it is the baby boomer mentality, or simply coming to the age of reason... either way, a high percent of homeowners in these active adult communities do cash purchases. This created a unique situation in these communities with the housing bust. Arizona was one of the hardest hit areas. We had the biggest gains and the baddest bust. Distressed properties (short sales and foreclosures) consisted of more than 75% of the homes on the market at one point. However in the age restrictive communities the distressed home sales were at less than 10% at that same time. Why? So many people who owned their home outright. You can't foreclose or short sale a home without a mortgage. The economic factor that affected the age restrictive communities was the stock market. As savings for upcoming retirement dwindled, many in the workforce committed to keep working a few years longer, and postponed the retirement move. That combined with the lower price of their current homes. They were left in a position of having to wait before they could progress to their retirement dreams.

Financially not everyone can purchase with cash. **Standard financing** is available for purchasing a home in any of these communities. Talk with your Realtor® to find a well qualified mortgage lender to explore your options.

The last options is a Home Equity Conversion Mortgage (HECM) commonly known as a **Reverse Mortgage**. Wait, hear me out... this isn't like the old ones. The whole loan program was revamped and is now insured and falls under the Federal Housing Administration (FHA), a division of US Housing and Urban Development (HUD). You can use this loan similar to a refinancing, or as a loan to purchase your home. You put a cash down payment, and the balance is paid by the lender. Just like a normal home purchase. The difference is, you don't make a mortgage payment ever. You are the owner of your home and as long as you live in your home as your primary residence, keep current with taxes, insurance and homeowner association fees (like any other loan) The difference is, you live there and don't make any mortgage payments. The interest gets added to the loan amount each month and increases the loan value over time.

How can I get a HECM?
One person purchasing or refinancing needs to be a minimum of 62 years of age. The loan amount will be based on the youngest borrower.

What happens after we pass on with the property?
The house can be purchased by your heirs for the current amount of the loan. If you have lived a long life, and have enjoyed your home to the point where the home loan is greater than the current value of the property, your heirs can either hand the property over to the lender, or purchase the property for 95% of appraised value.

What if I want to sell my home down the road?

Your house can be sold, just like any other home. The proceeds of the sale will pay of the balance of the loan, and any remaining proceeds will be yours, just like a normal sale. If the loan balance is greater than the current value, you can give the property back to the lender with no impact to you or your credit.

How long does it take for the loan value to increase over the home value?

This was one of the first questions I asked! There is no specific timeframe. It depends on property appreciation values, your age (which determines loan percent), price of your home at the time of the loan, interest rates etc. Let's just give an example... With the youngest borrower at 70 years of age, and a 300,000 purchase price, it will be an estimated 10-15 years before the loan balance will equal or exceed the home value.

Can I go to any lender to get a HECM loan?

The loan is an FHA loan, but not all lenders are familiar with the Home Equity Conversion Mortgages. Ask your Realtor® for a referral to a knowledgeable and experienced Reverse Mortgage Loan Officer.

Can I use a HECM loan to purchase a new build home?

Yes you can! The builder will have incentives tied to using their builder, and those incentives usually make more financial sense to use their lender than using any other lender. So start with the builders preferred lender. If they don't know about, or know how to do a HECM loan for purchase on a new construction property, go back to the builder's representative and negotiate getting the incentive they offered for using their lender and use one who has the experience with the HECM for purchase loans

BONUS CHAPTER 9

ESTATE PLANNING

By Leanne B. Martin

Welcome to the world of estate planning. In this chapter I will give an overview of some basic estate planning concepts. However, please note that laws vary from place to place, and there are too many particular rules, concepts, and circumstances to name them all here. Please use this as a general guide and then seek professional help for your own particular planning.

What is "Estate Planning?"

Estate planning is also known as "Legal Life Planning," Generally speaking, estate planning is deciding what you want to happen to your things and to your loved ones when you are no longer able to take care of them. Also, some aspects of estate planning may affect your own life, as we will discuss later.

Why do I need an estate plan?

We all know avoiding estate planning will not stop you from needing it - whether tomorrow or 20 years from now. But since no one knows when that day will arrive, the responsible thing to do is put your affairs in order sooner than later. This effort is primarily not for yourself, but for those you love. What would happen to your things and to everyone around you if you were suddenly gone? What would happen if you were no longer able to care for yourself? What would happen to your business and clients? What would happen to your pets? There may be all sorts of confusion and unintended results if you die without an estate plan. This is especially true for non-traditional family units, second marriages, troubled children, and such.

What is a will?

A will is a written document in which a person describes how he/she wants his/her estate managed and distributed after death. The requirements for preparation of this document are identified in state law.

What happens if I die without a will?

If you die without a will, this is called "intestacy." If you die intestate, the government has a plan for you. Each state has its own rules about who will inherit your assets, who will handle your probate estate as Executor or Personal Representative, and who will take care of your dependents (children or incapacitated adults) and their money through a guardianship or conservatorship. In general, expect all your assets to go to your spouse or, if you have no living spouse, to your children or, if no living children, to your parents, etc. If the state's list of succession ends with no one alive to take your money, then the state will keep it (it will "escheat" to the state). Thankfully, this rarely happens.

What if my estate is really small?

Each state has different rules, but if you have a small estate it might qualify for transfer without a traditional probate. Title may be able to be transferred by affidavit, instead.

Why might "no plan" be a bad plan?

There are several reasons why the state's plan might not be good.

1. It takes time. Usually a probate won't be started until after your death certificate is ready – which could take weeks (remember, this may vary by state). Meanwhile, someone could need access to an account but be frozen out of it. Bill collectors could start harassing your loved ones. Time sensitive things could fall through the cracks. Relatives could start crawling out of the woodwork and take things before anyone has authority to secure the house. You get the idea.

2. Who will take it upon himself/herself to petition the court to become your Personal Representative? That person may be required to post an expensive bond first. Can he/she afford to get that? Is his/her credit score good enough to get a bond? Controlling relatives may end up fighting each other for this job (this fight will mean more time in court and higher legal fees). Or perhaps worse, what if no one steps forward for the job? If no one voluntarily takes on this job, or cannot qualify for this job, a professional fiduciary will need to be hired/appointed, and that can get quite expensive.

3. There could be problems with your heirs. (An heir is someone with a right to inherit. A devisee is a person benefiting under a will. For simplicity, I will refer to both as "heir."). What if someone is not capable of handling money well or has a drug addiction? He'd still receive his share of the money with no restrictions or assistance. What if you have a long lost brother and you don't know if he's alive or dead – how long will your probate be held open while someone spends time and money to track him down? What if you have a dear friend you always wanted

to have a piece of art she admired? Unfortunately, friends are not part of the state's plan.

Is Probate a dirty word?

I hear this all the time on the radio: "do you really want your estate to go through … Probate?" It sounds so scary. Do you really know what probate is? Probate is a structured way to make sure your debts are paid, your assets distributed, and your dependents are taken care of. Probate is handled by your state's court system. Yes it takes time, but not necessarily a problematic amount of time. Yes it costs money, but not always a huge amount of money. It doesn't suspend all activity until it is final – things can start to happen (and should happen) soon after the probate is filed.

If you die intestate, or if you die with just a will, your estate will probably have to go through probate. I say probably because some people just don't need it. For example, if your only asset is a bank account and you held it jointly with your spouse, then a probate is not needed to give the account to your spouse.

Are there any concerns with probate?

1. It takes time. Expect it to take 4-16 months (it varies widely state to state). It could go longer, depending on circumstances.
2. Probate filings at court are public record. Someone can look at those files to learn who died and when, who may be receiving money, and how much money is in play. When people are known to be grieving and vulnerable, they can be targets of heavy sales pressure or fraud.
3. The expenses of probate (appraisers, professional fiduciaries, administration fees, legal fees…) will reduce the worth of your estate and so your heirs will receive a smaller amount than you'd expect. A good rule of thumb for probate costs is 3-8% of the value of your estate. The

costs could go higher, of course. If a professional fiduciary is involved, that could cost $100 an hour or more. If a relative decides to fight the probate administration for any reason, legal fees will increase.

4. What if some of the assets are not located? If the probate has closed and assets are located later, the probate may need to be re-opened. If they are not located and claimed within a certain amount of time, they will be taken or held by the state. Each state has its own law on what it will do with unclaimed property or funds.

What if I have real estate in more than one state?

Your Personal Representative may also need to open an ancillary probate in the other state in order to transfer ownership of that property. If you have all real estate in a living trust, an ancillary probate should not be needed.

Do I need a will or trust if I'm holding all my assets jointly with someone else?

You've been thinking ahead – good for you. But what if you and the other joint owner die at the same time? There is another problem you may not have considered. What if a creditor of your joint owner wants to garnish the account for payment because, after all, his/her name is on the account? If you want to fight the garnishment you'll have a lawsuit on your hands.

What about beneficiary designations?

If you have a life insurance policy or a retirement account, you likely have listed a beneficiary to receive the funds when you die. You need to review this periodically to make sure you still want that person to be the beneficiary. Problems arise if: you get divorced, the beneficiary has already died, you've lost track of the beneficiary's whereabouts, or the beneficiary is a minor child.

For instance, if the beneficiary is a minor child then there may still need to be a probate. A professional fiduciary may be appointed to watch over the child's money, and the child's guardian/parent may need to report annually on their use of that money for the child. What was put in place to protect the child's money from waste or theft can certainly be a hassle for whoever is taking care of the child. Then, at the tender age of 18, the adult child would receive all of the money. Not every 18 year old is wise enough to manage a large sum of money. So you can see that relying on a beneficiary designation can lead to unwanted consequences.

What is a trust?
A trust is an agreement with yourself to hold assets in the name of the trust for the benefit of beneficiaries. The Grantor (you) gives control over his/her assets to the Trustee (maybe you, maybe someone else) to manage those assets for the good of the listed beneficiaries (probably you and then others). When you hear the word "trust" that commonly means a living trust, set up and managed during your lifetime. A testamentary trust is set up in a will and created after death.

A trust can control who makes management decisions, when certain people receive their funds or under what circumstances they receive it. A trust can have detailed arrangements for taking care of your dependents. Depending on the type of trust, it may protect your assets from probate, predators, creditors, bankruptcy, divorce and taxes. A living trust can be useful for both your incapacity and death.

Are all trusts the same?
Trusts are as varied as people. What would work for one family might be inappropriate for another. Trusts can be short-lived or go

on for generations. Trusts can be revocable or irrevocable. They can be separate or joint.

What are some differences between wills and living trusts?

- Generally speaking, estate planning with a will costs most of its money after you die, because of the expense of probate.
- Estate planning with a trust costs most of its money when the document is prepared. If operated properly it can avoid the probate process, saving money.
- It usually costs less to write a will than a trust.
- Taking a will through probate requires attention to certain deadlines that must be met.
- Trusts are more flexible in their timing – fast or slow.
- With a will, the Personal Representative takes control after appointment by the probate court.
- With a trust, the Trustee can bring someone in as Co-Trustee while they are alive, for a smooth transition.

Do I need a trust to avoid estate taxes?

Assets passing through both a will and a basic living trust are subject to estate taxes. The good news is the federal estate tax only applies if the estate is larger than about $5 million ($5.49 million at the time I wrote this chapter). If taxes are a concern, you may be interested in a more complex form of trust. Obviously, if you have questions about taxes you'll want to speak with a professional.

If I have a trust, does that mean no one can fight over it?

People can always fight, but it may be a bit harder to fight a trust than a will.

If I have a trust do I still need a will?
Yes! You will need what is called a "pour-over" will so that if somehow some asset didn't make it into the trust, it can then be transferred (poured) into the trust.

Can there be any problem with Trusts?
One big problem commonly seen is failure to fully fund the trust. Maybe you put a lot of things in the name of the trust but bought something new in your own name. Some people are so relieved to have the trust done they just place it in a cabinet and forget to change title to anything.

How often should I review my estate plan?
It is a good idea to look over your estate plan at least every three years, in case there are changes in circumstances or changes in the law.

Does it matter where I create my estate planning documents?
You should prepare and sign your documents in your home state. If you move, I recommend you have an attorney review your documents for any possible problems. For instance, if you move from a community property state to a common law state, the effect of your will may be different than you expect.

Is there any other type of planning I should consider?
You should consider powers of attorney and a living will/health care directive (your instructions for end of life decisions). You may also want to consider life insurance, mortgage insurance, and prepaid burial plans. Having some or all of these in place will make life much easier for you or your loved ones.

What is a power of attorney?

A power of attorney gives someone else the power to make decisions for you. Definitely choose someone very trustworthy to take on that task. Consider creating a power of attorney for financial, health care, and mental health care decisions. Powers of attorney can be crafted to take effect immediately or when you become incapacitated.

Without powers of attorney, someone may have to petition the court for appointment as your guardian (to take care of your person) or conservator (to take care of your money) if you become incapacitated. This takes time. The court may or may not grant the request. Other relatives can fight over this. An expensive professional could be appointed instead, who may not care about what is really in your best interest (for example, he might insist you be placed in a less desirable care home in order to save money).

One important reminder – you must sign powers of attorney while you are still mentally competent. Otherwise by the time you really need them, it will be too late.

Now you can see there are many factors to consider when estate planning. If you need help thinking it through, I encourage you to seek assistance. Do not put this off for "some day." Your family will thank you for caring enough to plan for them.

ABOUT THE AUTHORS

Irene Jenkins Hammond is a very determined and very talented woman. She was one of those little girls who are born 40 years old, has never met a stranger and truly likes people. I cannot remember her ever disliking a person, child or adult. She even liked a giant Dalmatian who took a chunk out of her leg. Language has never been a barrier, might slow things down a bit, but never a deterrent. Her Dad is a gregarious Leo and she believes she belongs on stage right next to him. She was what was called "slow" in her early school years, she refused to write. Just plain refused. She was in 8th grade before we learned she was dyslexic and the b,p,d,q & o all looked alike. We were so fortunate to find a great school for her in our own neighborhood. In no time she was up to grade level and her last semester in high school made the A honor roll! Very determined, and very talented. Her Bachelor degree was in Computer Information Systems. She next graduated from the Ft. Lauderdale Art Institute with a photography degree.

Over the years she had several jobs, mostly summarized as being the boss's right hand. She was working for a mortgage broker when I begged her to get her real estate license and help me out, even just on weekends. She took to Real Estate like it was created and waiting for her arrival. The new build world was exploding in the Phoenix Valley of the Sun and we eased into a niche market working with Active Adults and 55+ communities. She met and married Rick, bought a home down the street from Mom and the rest follows in her book.

Mom, Claudina Jenkins

Leanne B. Martin was born in Pennsylvania and moved with her family to Arizona at the age of 11. She has a B.S. in General Business from Arizona State University (ASU) and a J.D. from the Sandra Day O'Connor College of Law at ASU. After admission to the Arizona bar in 1993, Leanne worked as an administrative law judge for the City of Phoenix and as an Assistant Attorney General for Arizona prior to going into private practice. She has been a partner at Golston & Martin, P.L.L.C. since 2011. Leanne currently works out of her office in Mesa, Arizona. The areas of emphasis in her practice are family law (divorce, custody, child support) and estate planning/probate (wills, trusts, powers of attorney).

Leanne is married and the mother of two teenagers – a boy and a girl. In her free time she enjoys everything relating to music (listening, singing, playing instruments, composing), cooking, reading, and writing.